Behind Baren:

<u>Escaping for family</u>

How far will you go to save you family?

Escaping for family

Behind Bars, Volume 1

Jens Van Wolput

Published by Jens Van Wolput, 2024.

While every precaution has been taken in the preparation of this book, the publisher assumes no responsibility for errors or omissions, or for damages resulting from the use of the information contained herein.

ESCAPING FOR FAMILY

First edition. December 24, 2024.

ISBN: 979-8230690405

Written by Jens Van Wolput.

"We may have our differences, but nothing's more important than family."

Author's story

I have been in love with reading and making stories for years, I made my first story at age 6 and have never stopped since. Now after 20 years my first book is out and ready to be read by you. I hope you enjoy it as much as I enjoyed writing it. I also want to inform you that there is a big chance that there are mistakes in this book and I want to apologize for them, I want to prove that limited language skills should not stop you from achieving your dream of publishing a book, with enough passion anything is possible!

· · · ·

I also hope to pass on my love for stories and bring people back to reading, because reading a book is escaping from real life and enjoying the masterpiece of our minds.

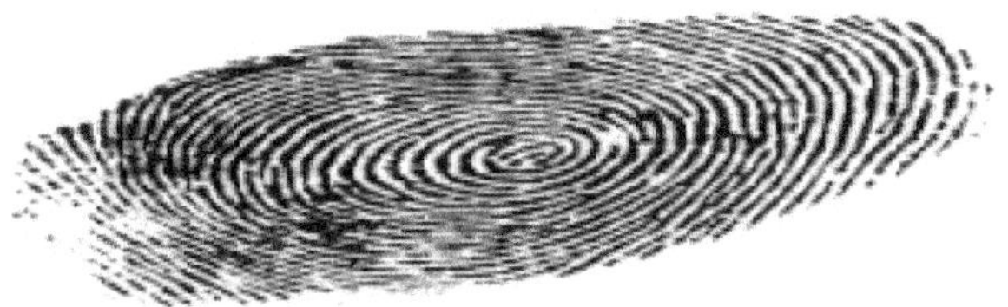

Chapter 1

Zéni looked into the black hole she had created over the past few days, it had been difficult to do it unnoticed in a room of eight people, but she had succeeded and she was quite proud of that.

As she stood there, Zéni was contemplating everything from the past two months, how everything had seemed so easy until disaster struck and she was arrested. She was locked in a human-unworthy room and there she had been for two months now.

It had all started with that stupid deal that went wrong, a small mistake by the buyer and she was stopped by an undercover cop. Zéni already had a feeling she should have walked down the other street and knew it all when the man followed her and stopped her at the corner to ask for something, but by then it was already too late.

She was whisked away to the police station a hundred yards away. She still found it ironic that most deals happen right under the nose of the police station. 'The best deals are always the ones that happen right under the cops' noses, they don't expect it and start focusing more on other places' someone had once told her and to this day it had always been right. When she was brought into the cell she had already resigned herself to her fate, someday it had to come, she knew, and better that it happened now than when she was old and had no future when she got out.

After two hours in the small cell with an aluminum toilet and a brick bed with a worn blanket, the officer came to the door again. "Ma'am, your lawyer is here, we are going to start your interrogation.

She got Zéni out of the cell and gave her back her shoes, without laces this time, and escorted her to the interrogation room where a woman was already sitting.

'Good evening ma'am, my name is Valerie Janssen, I am your lawyer. I have been called by the police to assist you with your questioning,' after which she turned to the officer. 'I would now like to have the half hour to discuss with my client, I will get you when we are done.' With these words, the agent, clearly irritated that she was being pointed at by a lawyer, turned and walked out of the room.

"So, Mrs. Valler is it?

'Right, Zéni Valler.'

'Okay, I'm going to ask you some questions to get to know you better. Then we will discuss how we are going to do this interrogation, is that okay with you?'

'Yes, sure master.'

'Okay, what is your date and place of birth?'

"I was born on March 3, 1997 and in Brasschaat.

'Okay, and your living in?'

'I live in Frans de l'Arbrelaan 25, 2170 in Merksem.'

'Okay, and you got caught with?'

'I got caught on the street for cannabis, but there's still some cocaine and ecstasy pills at home.'

"Do you have any idea how much?

"No.

"And this is yours?

'Yes, a lady may earn a little extra money, right?'

'Yes, of course, but better not this way, because now you are sitting here.'

To that, Zéni had no counter answer. To each his own, she thought to herself.

Ms. Janssen looked up from her papers and looked Zéni in her eyes. She had big blue eyes, eyes you could trust if they didn't belong to a lawyer.

'Can I ask something right now? I'm not going to write this down but they're going to ask it. What is a woman doing in that world? It's a man's world, you hear that everywhere.'

'That's exactly why it's perfect for a woman, they get everything done.' After those words, she saw a small smile around the corners of Mrs. Janssen's mouth.

'Okay, what I suggest is that you just don't say anything. We don't know what they have and the officers don't know what you have, you understand?'

Zéni nodded her head. Sounded logical, she thought

'So you just don't say anything about it now, not even saying 'won't say', or 'won't answer'. Your right to remain silent is literally to remain silent, are you ready?

She stood up straight and went to get the agent, who came immediately and sat down behind her PC.

'Ms. Valler, I am going to read you your rights for a moment and then we will begin. Your lawyer is not allowed to intervene in the interrogation, she is only here to consult together, which you have just done. She is also here to see that your rights are not violated. You also have the right to remain silent and you can consult with your lawyer once, you will get fifteen minutes for that, understood?

'Yes, plain and simple.'

'Okay, could you please state your name, date and place of birth and residence?'

'Zéni Valler, I was born on March 3, 1997 in Brasschaat and I live at Frans de l'Arbrelaan 25, 2170 in Merksem.'

'You were caught selling in narcotics, what do you want to say about it?'

Silence.

'In your apartment was found 300 grams of cocaine, 20 grams of cannabis and 20 pills of ecstasy, what do you want to say about it?'

Silence.

"Who were you working with?

This question worked like a red rag on a bull and she flew out.

'IS IT BECAUSE I'M A WOMAN THAT YOU THINK I CAN'T WORK ALONE? I'M WORTH MORE THAN SOME MEN AND I CAN MAKE THEM DO WHATEVER I WANT!

'Madam, would you please calm down a bit or this is done.'

'Okay. Mrs. Janssen, thank you for coming, please take me back to my cell.'

'If you do this I will put in your report that you were uncooperative and the investigating judge is not going to like that.'

'Madam, if you do this I can declare that this interrogation is annulled. My client did not refuse to cooperate, she invoked her right to remain silent and then did what you asked and went back to her cell. My client is not at fault so perhaps we had better leave it at that.

For a moment, the officer didn't know what to do anymore and then went outside to get a copy of the statements.

After signing the interrogation, Zéni was taken back to her cell and fell into a dreamless sleep.

When she woke up she didn't know how long she had slept though it didn't feel that long.

'Are you getting up? Then they will take you away to the headquarters,' said the agent standing at the door.

"What time is it?

'It's now six in the morning, you're here for seven hours.'

Zéni stood up and the door opened. She stepped back into the lace-up shoes, but she didn't notice much. Her head was only on sleeping, which she found odd because she had finally slept a little.

Standing in front of the building were two officers in full uniform and a face she could not remember afterwards. She got into the back of the police car with her hands cuffed in front of her and was taken away in a daze.

The drive didn't take long. It's Sunday, everyone is snuggling in their beds at home, she thought slowly to herself. When they got there she got out and was escorted inside where an old desk stood with an even older man behind it. 'Please sit down on the bench, take off your coat and wait a moment,' said one of the officers escorting her.

Both agents walked to the desk and filled out documents she didn't know what they were and the agents whispered among themselves. After a while, she heard something to her right and discovered an open door with a male officer in the doorway. He was a large man with his right arm full of tattoos and a thick black beard combined with a bald head which was a funny sight, Zéni thought.

"Please come this way, ma'am," he said, beckoning her. Uncomfortably, Zéni stepped up and walked to the door and went inside. Once she was inside there was a machine on the left with a screen upright like a computer but also a screen flat where the keyboard would normally be. She didn't understand anything about it, there were feet drawn on the floor against the wall and on the opposite side a small camera standing on a desk where a female agent sat. The agent seemed taken straight from an cop series on TV and looked more like an actress whose job it was to convey the general English language to the viewers.

'Good morning miss, please get to your feet with your face straight to the camera,' the woman said with a trace of a Dutch accent that made it not simple to determine where she was coming from. Zéni got to her feet and looked straight into the camera.

'Good, now turn to your left for a moment please.'

Zéni turned to the left.

'Perfect, you are doing very well, now just a moment to your right please.'

Zéni turned to the right.

'Okay, very well done girl, now go get the fingerprint.'

Apparently, the machine that Zéni did not recognize was the fingerprint machine.

'Just put your index finger on it and wait,' the officer with the tattoos said.

Thus they went off all the fingers of both hands along with the entire palm and, to Zéni's surprise, the sides of her hands as well.

Eventually this too was done and she was taken to her own little cell via an elevated platform that ran through the back of the office in the other room to the cells, this one was made entirely of aluminum and it was bloody hot.

Very good, at least then I can use my sweater as a pillow, she thought, laughing, and she was surprised that she didn't have more anxiety about the future to come.

She lay down and immediately fell asleep again in the greenhouse of a cell.

When she woke up she was disoriented for a while and lay in her own sweat. After a while she recognized her cell with the toilet in the corner and a cheese sandwich at the door. Like a hungry hyena, she went for it and shoved it into her mouth almost in one go.

When she finished the sandwich, she heard the door and when it opened, Zéni had to avert her eyes for a moment for the light coming from the hallway.

'Come out, put your shoes on and we'll cuff you.' Yet another officer came to get her.

She did as they asked and put her hands in front of her belly to cuff them.

'Now walk forward and sit down on the bench.'

Zéni meekly followed what she was told, and once on her bench she was joined by three more men who watched her very closely.

One of the men had a thin beard, short hair that stood up in spikes with blond color, jeans and a black T-shirt.

The other two both had no hair, one of the two men had a ring beard and they were both wearing black sweatshirts and sweatpants.

'They are all here, we are ready for transport.'

'Transportation? Where are we going?" the man with blond hair asked.

'We will take you to the Palace of Justice, where you will be told whether you will be further detained or released.'

They were divided into a van that had six different compartments, with Plexiglas between each compartment and a separate door to each compartment. Zéni sat in the back at the window so she could look outside. Fortunately, the windows were tinted so you couldn't see in from outside.

They went up the lane and were soon on the ring of Antwerp to the South and entered the Palace through the back where they were again unloaded. They got out and went through a double door, down the stairs and then to the right where they entered a large room with a concrete "bench" in the middle to sit on.

When everyone was inside, the door closed with a big bang and there they stood, no one said anything but everyone looked at her She stood in a corner so she could not be surprised from behind and looked at everyone calmly and calculatingly. She was not afraid because she had done martial arts before and knew that men have one weakness that hangs between their legs.

After a while, the door opened and a female officer appeared and watched everything. 'Mohammed Kud, come here and walk to cell 3.'

The bald man with no ring beard walked up to her, took one last look at Zéni and then walked on.

The woman waited a moment until the man was in his cell and then continued. "Kristof Lauwers, come here and walk through to cell 10.

The man with blond hair walked on and disappeared through the door.

'Zéni Valler, come here and walk through to cell 13.'

Zéni walked to the door and saw a very long corridor with thick blue doors with windows in them and shutters in front of them every few feet between each other. She walked past thirteen of them and joined the officer who stood there, uncuffed her and she then looked into the cell.

A bench you couldn't lie on and that was it. Everything was concrete and old and dirty. She went inside and the door closed, then the fear came. She had never suffered from claustrophobia or anxiety attacks, but there in that "cell" they both came very quickly. There was nothing of fresh air and the brick bench was so slippery she slipped off. She lay down and tried to sleep which of course now she couldn't. She cursed. "Why have I been sleeping so much for the past hour? Compared to this, the warm ugly little cell she came from was a four-star hotel.

After sitting in that cell for hours, she desperately needed to go to the bathroom and started banging on the door. After what seemed like an eternity, an officer finally came and took her to the exact same kind of cell only where the couch had been turned into a toilet, the dirtiest toilet she had ever seen.

She put toilet paper on the seat to avoid touching it and squatted slightly above it and did her errand. That's a first time I've had to do it that way, too, she thought, washing her hands in an aluminum sink. She knocked on the door and had to wait a long time again, once back in her cell she did what she did all the time: tried to sleep.

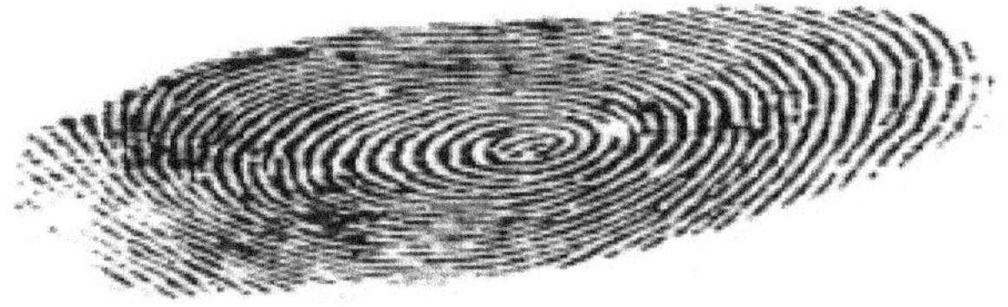

Chapter:2

The hatch of the door opened and there came the pockmarked face of a cop. The door opened and the cop came to stand in the doorway. 'Come over here. Turn around and we'll cuff you. '

Once handcuffed, Zéni went with the agent, down the other side of the corridor than she had come, to two elevators. When she got there, she looked up at the agent for a moment. Apart from his hook nose, he had a thick gray mustache, making his nose stand out even more, and thin gray hair combed to one side of his face.

The door of the right elevator opened. Stepping in, the officer pressed a button and showed his badge against a badge reader. The elevator climbed steadily to its final destination.

They got off the elevator and went down a long corridor with a door every few feet with signs on it like "Room of First Council" and more she couldn't remember after that. After three or four doors the officer knocked and went inside before anyone could even say anything. Inside, she saw two tables right in front of her that together formed a hexagon against each other. When she looked to her left, she saw two large desks set against each other in an L-shape and two chairs, one of which was already occupied by her lawyer. Behind the desks sat directly in front of her an older man with a bald spot on top of his head and around it pitch black hair and a thin beard of the same color.

To his right, a woman was typing diligently on the computer in front of her. Zéni couldn't get a good look at her because of the stack of documents between them.

'Have a seat,' the man said in a brutal voice. She sat down on the only chair that was free, was uncuffed and thanked the officer with a head nod.

'Mrs. Valler, I'm investigating judge Maes, I'm here to determine if i will send you to prison or if you will be released with or without conditions.' He looked up at her for a moment and sighed. 'You were arrested on February 8 in our lordship's year 2020 on suspicion of selling narcotics, how do you plead?'

'What you found you found huh sir, there's no getting around that.'

Maes looked up in surprise for a moment and then said to the clerk to his left, 'Note that Mrs. Valler confessed that the drugs were at her home. And who did the drugs belong to, ma'am?

Silence.

"Are you prepared to say something about what we found, ma'am?

Silence.

'Note that Mrs. Valler does not wish to cooperate and I hereby sentence her to jail. Madam, you will be taken to jail, you will appear again in five days and I hope that by then you will have been able to put your thoughts in order and we can move forward. Do you have anything to add, Madam Advocate?

Janssen stood up and briefly looked everyone in the room in the eye to make sure she had the attention of the room. 'Dear Mr investigating judge, we feel it is the right decision to send Madam to prison for five days but not for her to think but for you to take a look at her file as I did last evening.

Mrs. Valler has been an orphan all her life, mom died at birth, dad never showed up, she's gone shelter in and shelter out and when she turned eighteen she was just thrown out on the street by the state. Now you have to tell me what usually comes from a girl going through this. She paused for a moment to reinforce her words. 'Most of them you can find behind glass in the Red Street in Antwerp, but not my client. My client made sure she could do what the state was actually supposed to do, take care of her. I would ask that you keep this in mind the next time a young woman stands here who had no other choice but to survive.'

Silence, it had never been so quiet in the room, Zéni thought. The only sound came from the clerk's keyboard, which touched her keys as Beethoven did with a symphony.

The lawyer walked to the table where there was a paper, signed it and said to Zéni, "I'll come see you when you're inside and we'll talk further, keep strong, you'll be out in no time.

Zéni was helped upright by the agent and led to the table.

'If you would just sign this paper ma'am, it's a copy of the judgment.'

She signed and was captivated again.

The way back happened in a happy state. Even though she had to go to jail, the lawyer was right. She dared to blame the state and that was what was needed, there was hope for the case.

Back in her little cell it became too much for her for a moment and the memories resurfaced. Her mother had died and her father had bailed, well that was what the foster parents always said anyway. Three had come and gone, everywhere she had run away or had done something that kept her from being there. From the age of thirteen she had been on the streets and stealing and yet she regretted nothing because what is life without risk.

When she woke up, her door was opened.She already could not remember falling asleep but her cheeks were wet with tears. Annoyed, she wiped them away; she hadn't cried in ten years and wouldn't begin to either.

They were put in the same car again in the same place and drove away. They drove out of the Palace over the slates, street in street out, so many turns that Zéni could not follow and before she knew it they were in front of a green gate on a street she did not recognize.

The gate opened and the car drove in. The men were unloaded and brought in through a large door; Zéni had to stay put and wait until everyone was inside.

Finally they came to get her and even before she could ask anything the officer said. "Be glad you weren't there, those men were already undressing you in their dreams.

She could only agree that if they had had the chance it would have already happened.

The walk from the car to the door was short but still Zéni had enough time to look around. The building was built of old brick and had cracks in the mortar everywhere, every window had white bars in front of them, a truly depressing sight.

On her way to the door, she passed a small white shack with all the lockers in front of it, and as she stared at it, she saw a cop put his gun in the locker and lock the locker.

The agent opened the large door and pushed Zéni inside and closed the door again behind the two of them. Where they now stood inside was a sort of lock with the door behind them and a grille door in front of them, a buzz indicated that the door was loose and so the agent opened it.

Inside, she saw a small desk in front of her, a glass cage to her right and three doors. She was taken to one of the doors which appeared to be a waiting room. Once inside, she heard voices in the hallway and saw that an older woman had sat down behind the desk and was talking to the officer. What they were saying was unintelligible and after a few moments she beckoned to Zéni.

She was stripped of her restraints. "Put your index finger on the little screen. There was a small round ball precisely attached to the desk in the top of which was a red screen.

She put her finger on it and waited. "What is your name, child?" the woman asked in a motherly voice.

'Zéni Valler.'

'Okay, just take your finger off and walk on the left to the first door, my colleague will help you then.'

Zéni looked at the path she indicated and was surprised. There were three of those barred doors, about six doors on either side of the corridor and all of them has posters of old prison movies next to them.

She walked down the hallway and stopped at the first door on the left; what she saw inside almost made her smile.

There was a man sitting there, well she thought so anyway. The small room was divided in half with a giant Plexiglas wall. And she saw a small man on the other side in a cluttered room full of documents and a desk with a computer crammed into it.

'Ms. Valler, welcome to the Antwerp arrest house, would you please stand against the wall and look up into the camera?'

Zéni stood with her back against the wall and looked for a camera, only she didn't see one.

'Perfect, please sit down,' the man said in a sawing voice. 'I am the clerk of the Antwerp arrest house, as mentioned, this is only an arrest house. If you are convicted, you will be transferred to another prison where you will serve your sentence. If you would just sign this. The clerk placed a paper in front of Zéni who began to read it.

"It *is hereby confirmed that Zéni Valler is deprived of her liberty for selling narcotics whether in group or otherwise.*

Zéni Valler will be remanded in custody for at least five days after which she must appear before the council chamber where further arrest or release will be decided.

Was signed by.

investigating judge suspect

Maes"

'Just sign under suspect?

'Yes please, and put your name with it because in most signatures you can't find a name again.'

Zéni signed the paper and handed it back to the clerk.

"Must you have a copy?

'No, I can't do anything with it anyway.'

'Then you may go. Out the door and to the right.'

Zéni stepped outside again into the hallway with many doors, went to the right and passed three of them before she realized that they were all rooms to meet lawyers. When she got to the last door on the left, she saw a nameplate with "accountant" on it and had to restrain herself from laughing. With all the criminals here they had better put the accountants further away, soon all the money would be gone. As she continued walking through the last grille door, she saw in front of her a glass wall with three doors. To her left was a sort of waiting room with wooden benches on either side, to her right were two doors with a metal detector between them.

She walked on to the metal detector where an officer was waiting, this one smaller than her but broadly built, with a haircut that belonged in the military.

'Just walk through the metal detector and enter the door in front of it.'

She walked through the metal detector that remained silent, turned around again and sat down in the room the officer pointed out. The room was filthy, the only window there was covered with a wooden board bolted into the wall every few inches. The benches on either side of the room were made of wood and showed the necessary burn marks, the wall was full of texts from nationalities to snitches and where they worked. On the right side of the room was a red door with a shutter in it at eye level, through which you couldn't see anything along this side.

The whole environment made Zéni realize where she had ended up and that she had to be very careful what she said to whom, because while this may only be a detention house, this was the first place every criminal from Antwerp ended up and she was only a young woman.

Later she could not tell how long she had sat there, reading the walls and pacing. After a while the door opened and a large man appeared in the doorway, he was a little set but had a friendly face.

He had thick hair combed back and a thin mustache. "Come inside and then wait. She went inside and stood in a triangular room with a door behind her, to her left and one in front of her that was open. Behind it she could see a pair of screen curtains dividing the room.

As the agent closed the door behind her, he beckoned her to move on. Once in the room, she saw another metal detector to her left, and she could also see that the screen curtains were actually shower curtains with the necessary shower attached.

'Walk through the metal detector and then wait a moment, a female officer will arrive to search you and afterwards you are going to have to take a shower.'

Indeed, when she walked through the metal detector and turned around, a female officer was already there, a woman who would probably be looked over by every inmate and perhaps the jailers as well.

She was small, had a pretty face with a little rocker nose, and firm breasts.

'Okay, now go to the shower and undress.'

She went to the shower and undressed.

'Just put everything on the wall so I can check it.'

She laid everything out nicely on the little wall, and the agent checked everything. First her black coat with brown faux pinks on the hood, then her red sweater and her white top, then followed by her jeans and socks.

When everything was checked, the agent put everything on a table behind her.

'Underwear you may also hang over the wall and then shower, if you look over the wall you will see your prison clothes.'

She pulled the curtain closed and Zéni was left alone in the shower in her underwear and for a moment she didn't know what to do. She stood there so vulnerable and for a moment she felt like a young girl of sixteen again when she did it the first time with her boyfriend. She had also felt as small and vulnerable then as she did now.

She undressed and laid her underwear on the wall, then turned on the shower and stood under the water. The water was nice and warm and for a moment she forgot all her worries, everything seemed to wash away together with the water in the drain of the shower and for a moment she wished she could wash away with it.

After the shower she put her underwear back on and looked at the table with the clothes she had been given, it was a pink T-shirt and gray pants that together formed the ugliest combination she had ever seen and against her will she put them on.

When she was dressed, she saw that the agent had sat down at the desk at the back of the room and she sat down across from it.

'Alright Ms. Valler, first I'm going to go over the rules with you. Here we have full respect for everyone no matter what gender, race, orientation or whatever. Understood?

'Yes, that's obvious.'

'You can go to church here, write doctor, go to the library and so on, for this you must fill out this bill, we call this a report card.'

She showed a bill that said "report card" at the top in print, with a black line below to divide the sheet, and below that was name, first name, cell number and date.

'Here you just fill in your name, your first name, your cell number and the date of the day you are going to drop it off, under that you just fill in your question and sign it at the bottom. You then drop this off at the sandwiches in the evening and they are going to answer your question as soon as possible. I got a paper bag here for you, everybody gets one here. I put some of those papers in there.'

Next to her was a brown paper bag that now held the report cards.

'There is also a landline phone on every cell, from the money in your account you can transfer money to make calls. With this card you get nine minutes free to call, every euro you transfer is worth nine minutes. On this form, again enter your name, first name, date and cell number, then in the box enter how many euros you want as call credit. Remember, the least is one euro so you cannot request less than nine minutes. Also, you must remember that money must already be in your account before you transfer it.'

She stuck a few of the "calling cards" in the paper bag.

'This is a welcome booklet, it says everything again just like the account number to put money in your account. Are you a smoker?'

That question surprised her a little, was she now offering her a cigarette?

'No, I don't smoke, thank you.'

'Okay, then you get six euros on your bill from us, if you were a smoker you got tobacco and leaves.'

She handed her a plastic card with the picture on it that she had had taken at the clerk's office and her name underneath. Now I'm officially a prison customer, she thought bitterly.

'This is your badge, you take it with you every time you leave your cell. If you lose it you will pay us ten euros. I am going to take you straight to your cell, inside you will find your blankets, towels and everything you need. In this bag you will also find a toothbrush, toothpaste, two small bottles of shampoo and a cube of soap.'

The agent stood up and waited for Zéni to grab the paper bag and follow her through the door. Once through the door, she was momentarily disoriented.

In front of her she saw a glass room like a fishbowl only this fishbowl was filled with computer screens and agents, clearly a control room. Around this control room to her right was a circular staircase to the next floor, to its right was a large grille door with a giant corridor with more doors in it than she could count.

Before Zéni could see more the agent preceded her to the floor above, on the wall flush with the stairs was a large graffiti drawing with the letters *"FAITH"* in purple on it. They walked up the stairs to the floor above which looked exactly the same as the one below and without waiting the agent walked on to the floor above so followed Zéni without looking around.

At the top of the third floor they had to stop for a moment because there was a grille door in front of the next staircase which allowed her to look around for a moment, here too was a fishbowl and a grille door with a long hallway behind it. She also saw another poster of an old prison movie *"alkatraz only one goes out"* it read with names she didn't know. Across the fishbowl she saw another grille door and part of what she thought was another long hallway.

The grille door opened and they went upstairs, again she saw a fishbowl there with an agent and several computer screens. They walked to the first large grille door she saw and waited there.

As they stood there for a moment, Zéni began to wonder what they were waiting for until she heard a buzzing and the agent opened the door. Apparently these doors were opened from the fishbowl, they walked down the corridor to the very back and stopped there.

The officer took a key from her pocket and inserted it into the keyhole and opened the door, Zéni stood in the doorway with her paper bag and looked inside. To her new cellmate and her room for at least five days. This is the new life, she thought to herself.

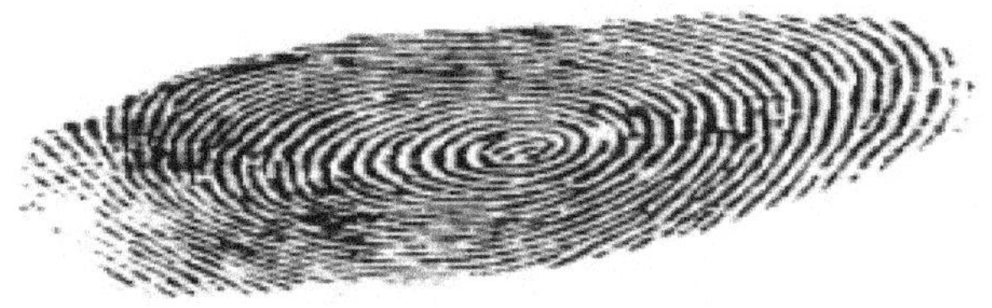

Chapter 3

The cell was about three meters by six meters, and on the wall opposite the door was a window with bars attached in front of it and a kind of metal lattice with all little holes so you couldn't throw anything through it.

Directly to her right was a large wooden cabinet divided in two with different compartments in it, the left one was already occupied so she briefly put her things in the right one. All over the cabinet was drawn and all kinds of writing.

Between the closet and the wall with the window was a bunk bed made of simple wood. The bottom bed was made up and belonged to her cellmate, on the top was a pile of things she thought were her blankets.

Opposite the bed against the wall was a heavy wooden table with two chairs and to its right was a small refrigerator with a small television set fixed to the wall above it.

On the other side of the table was a sink with a white shelf above and a dirty mirror full of scratches, still to the left of that was the toilet completely open to the rest of the cell. Zéni hadn't thought about that yet, and now that she saw it like this, she knew she wasn't going to use it right away.

Her cellmate got up from her bed; she was smaller than Zéni and narrower, too. 'Hey, my name is Amy. Up there is your bed, if I were you I would cover that up first because if they see that hasn't happened yet soon you will get disciplined and you really don't want that so early on.'

She lowered herself back onto the bed and let Zéni have her way for a moment, who then went to look at the pile on her bed.

The pile consisted of a thin blanket, a pillowcase, a pillow, a kitchen towel, a large and a small towel and then also a pillowcase to put over her mattress. Zéni began to make her bed and was fumbling with the pillowcase for over her mattress.

There, the elastic had been taken out, causing the corners to hang limply down and get in Amy's way.

When she saw that Zéni was groaning she took pity and went to help her. "First time for sure?

'Yes, does it stand out that much?'

'Yes, everyone who has been here before already knows this trick.' She took the two corners and tied a knot in them under the mattress. 'So now you can turn in your bed all you want, it won't run.' And when she saw Zéni watching, she added, 'I learned this from my previous cellmate who I spent one day with, she was transferred after her five days in observation here.'

'So this is not permanent?'

'No, after five days you'll appear again and if you have to stay then you'll go to the corridor next door there are those who are waiting for their second council chamber, or if they are stupid court of appeal.'

'Why if they are stupid?'

'Because if you are convicted after five days on a one-month stay here and you appeal and you lose that you are here for one month and two weeks, the weeks of your appeal don't count.'

While the two were chatting, Zéni had made her bed, and now she sat down briefly on the chair by the table. "And why are you sitting here?

'I'm here for burglary, twenty-three burglaries and only caught on one.'

'Wow, that's not bad.' Zéni could barely suppress the feeling of surprise.

'Yes, I agree. The trick is knowing if your victims are home or not. With the last one I was unlucky, flight was cancelled. And you, what are you here for?

'I got caught with drugs.'

'Ai, selling narcotics. First time in jail, huh? And already collided with police?'

"The lawyer says I have a lot of extenuating circumstances.

For the first time since Zéni had entered, she gave herself a moment to look around. The walls were painted in dirty beige with everything written everywhere. From Nazi signs to names and again many names of snitches.

She also looked briefly at the woman she would share a cell with for five days. As she had already seen, she was smaller and narrower than Zéni. She had a perfectly round face, blond hair and blue eyes. A real beauty who could turn many a man's head, even if that was not so difficult these days.

Zéni could also well imagine how perfect her figure would be even though you couldn't see it so well in those clothes. 'What does the daily schedule here actually look like, and what all can you do here?'

'At six in the morning they are at the door here shouting "GOOD MORNING", you don't have to respond to that but you do if they come by one hour later for the bins and medication. If you don't, they write it down, if it happens too much you have a problem. Then around nine o'clock I think they come with coffee, hot water and soup. Hot food is around noon and then around six we get sandwiches. She paused for a moment as she talked about the sandwiches. 'In fact, I think they're almost going to be there with the sandwiches. Also if you need papers like report cards. You have to ask for those at nine o'clock by the soup and drop them off at six by the sandwich. If you forget it then you can forget it for the day.'

When she heard the door open she looked up for a moment before grabbing from the cupboard two plates and two knives. "I also have an extra spoon, fork, bag and deep plate here for you, Zéni," she said as she handed her the plate.

She grabbed one bag of white bread even though Amy said she wanted to grab a brown one if Zéni preferred, who kindly thanked her for it. She wasn't hungry anyway. They both also got a pot of chicken curry and the door closed again. They sat down and Amy immediately flew at her sandwiches like she hadn't eaten in weeks.

When she finished, Zéni had not yet touched her sandwiches, and when she saw Amy's look she handed the jar of chicken curry to her.

'Wow thanks, if you get hungry later, there's a box of jam in the cupboard, we get it for free here every Saturday, as well as toilet paper. But I wouldn't eat that if I were you haha.'

They spent the rest of the evening watching TV, each on her own bed, and talking a bit, finding out that Amy had learned to steal from her ex-boyfriend and that she was indeed not averse to throwing her body into the fray. 'Tell you what, if the sex was good you have another bonus. If not, well then you have his stuff anyway, it's all insured anyway.'

'But how do you know which man to hit on?'

'Simple, give them booze. Men then start bringing up everything they have. Cars, paintings, their wife's jewelry.'

They had both laughed until their stomach muscles hurt and then stopped talking to watch the news where a woman was just talking about the indecision of ministers to form a government.

'By now we have been without a government for two hundred and thirty days, and will remain so for a while as long as NVA and P.S. do not want to cooperate,' they heard the woman say.

'Well, who is going to run the country they don't know, but whoever wants to make money they lock up without consultation. 'Welcome to Belgium,' Amy said, and Zéni could only agree.

When Zéni woke up she looked down where Amy was still sleeping, she herself had slept super badly. The mattress was thin and you could feel the wooden slats of the slatted base in your back, the pillow was so thin that you lay with your head down and got pain in your neck, not to mention the blanket you got there that was super thin.

She heard the door open and the officer who appeared in the doorway looked around for a moment and then called out "GOOD MORNING" and closed the door again.

'Oh well, that cop was in far too good a mood again. He must have heard that it's Friday's strike,' a voice suddenly sounded below her.

"What do you mean strike?

'Yes for a while now it's been strike every Friday and they must have heard it's this Friday again.'

"So what does that entail?

'Friday there is no shower, no walk, no canteen sharing, and so on so that's 24 hours in the cell.' Amy stood up stretched and walked to the bathroom. 'Can you pass me that little wooden slat that's on top of the cabinet?'

Zéni looked on the cupboard and saw two wooden shelves put together with hinges so that could be put in front of the toilet and give a little privacy between the one sitting on the toilet and the one standing by it.

She put the wooden shield in front of the toilet and Amy sat down, Zéni looked the other way and even though it was not a number two, she still found it very embarrassing to hear her pee and she decided to hold it up as long as she could.

The door opened again and there stood another officer along with two men in blue polo shirts and a cart with one jug with "coffee" written on it and one with "hot water" and in the middle a large one with yellow brown soup.

'Coffee, water, soup? Anyone have a few more bills? He said it like it was a recorded tape so devoid of intonation and feeling.

"Yes, two jugs of coffee, or do you prefer water, rookie?" said Amy with a smile.

'Yes, hot water delicious, especially without tea flavor,' Zéni laughed along, and she saw approval in Amy's eyes that she got the joke immediately.

'Yes ladies, then you must order tea huh. Here are the canteen sheets for today.' He handed over two A4 papers, filled the jugs and pulled the door shut again.

'Yes that one is in good spirits again, didn't you have to have soup?'

'Does it bother us then? He's on the other side of the door haha, and no in the morning I can't eat much anyway, only coffee is needed.'

'Yes I understand, if you want sugar, it's between the refrigerator and the wall in a white bag. Grab three for me if you want.'

Zéni went to look where she had said and indeed saw a white bag filled with sugar.

'Well, to sugar deprivation we certainly won't go,' she said as she handed Amy three lumps.

'Yes, the only thing we don't have here is milk. According to my previous cellmate, we only get half a gallon a week on Saturdays.'

'Doesn't matter, as long as there's sugar in it I'll get the coffee in.'

They sat down at the table together and for minutes there was silence as they enjoyed their coffee. As they sat there, Zéni was looking out through the bars and looking up at a wall that sloped on their wall.

The only way to see anything other than the wall was to stand right by the window and then you could see part of the square where they had the walk.

'Do you know yet when you're going to have your initiation thingy here?" asked Amy suddenly

'No, they didn't say anything about that. What does that mean, then?

First you go to the doctor, where they will see if you have tuberculosis. Then you go to the psychologist and you are called up to JWA, which is the social service here. Finally, you go to the director and he just says you have to stay here and if you have any questions about your stay.'

'Only when I can go home, but she can't decide that, can she?

'No, I'm afraid so haha.'

The day went on quietly, they each drank two more cups of coffee, washed the cups afterwards and went to watch TV.

After many hours, the door opened again and another officer came and stood in the doorway "VALLER?

"Yes, I am?

'Doctor.'

'Because you ask so sweetly.'

'You can keep that big mouth to yourself otherwise it's isolation.'

"Okay, sorry I'm coming. She got out of bed and put on her shoes.

"Badge?

"Yes. She showed the officer her badge.

'Okay fine,' he said after not even glancing at the badge. 'Just walk on over to my colleague over there.' And he pointed to a female officer further down the road.

"Just come over here and turn around," the officer said as she walked up.

She turned around and the officer searched her.

When it was in order, she and the agent went to the grille door, where they stayed for a moment waiting for a buzzing sound, the sign that the door was loose.

They went through the door and down the stairs where again was the grille door that you had to open with the key.

When the agent unlocked the door she escorted her to the fish bowl where a speaker hung. A "beep" sounded and the agent said, "Valler, Zéni. For the doctor.'

'Okay, let them go to the waiting room.'

The agent nodded to her colleague and turned to Zéni. 'All right, you go down the stairs to the lowest floor, there you will also find a speaker like this, you say you need to see the doctor and they will tell you where to go.'

Zéni went down the stairs and was looked at on every floor by every man she encountered. She had noticed before that with her muscular body she could make any man's head spin. And even though you couldn't see it in this outfit, she had already noticed that from how she walked people could quickly tell what kind of wood she was cut from, and the way she walked there every man saw that she had a beautiful body.

She came downstairs and went straight to the fishbowl, from the first corridor behind the barred door she heard, "Hey honey, come with me to my cell and I'll show you every angle.

Zéni looked to her right and saw a broad large man full of tattoos on his arms looking at her, the man did not look bad. He had short blond hair parted to the left and a beard that matched his face perfectly.

She walked to the bars but kept enough distance. "I don't think you're going to be able to handle that baby, I'll eat you with hair and skin.

'Come a little closer and I'll make you feel something.'

Zéni took a step closer but just as his hand shot forward to touch her breasts she took a step back, grabbed his hand and pulled.

His head banged hard against the bars but Zéni did not let go. Still holding the hand, she took a big step to the left, causing the arm to bend outward in a strange curve, and she could already see that it was broken in three places.

She let go of the arm and walked toward the speaker. 'Zéni Valler, doctor. And take that man at once, I think he has fallen,' she said pointing with her thumb at the fellow who just wanted to grope her.

There was chaos in the hallways, agents came running up and held Zéni against the glass walls of the fishbowl while holding her hands behind her back.

The man she had attacked was helped to his feet and taken to the doctor who was on the other side of the room behind another glass wall.

'You're going to regret this, just lock this savage in the cabin. I'll go see for myself in a few hours to see if she has regrets yet!'

"LOSE HER AND BRING HER TO ME, JEAN!" it suddenly sounded from behind Zéni so she couldn't see who was shouting it.

'Chief, didn't you see what she did?'

'I mostly saw what Stan did and this girl only protected herself. Isn't it your job to counter this? Maybe I should do an evaluation of your job here?'

'Yes chief, I'll take her to your office in a moment,' the man said submissively, then turned to Zéni. 'You are lucky to have such powerful friends, girl. How do you know the director so well that he stands up for you?'

Before she could answer, she was whisked away to the other side of the fishbowl, past the doctor's waiting room where everyone was watching her.

They stopped in front of two offices and Zéni was pushed into the right one of the two. The office was cozy.

A desk was right in front of her with a MacBook on it and an expensive brown leather chair behind it, there were several green filing cabinets probably full of the prisoners' files.

In the corner was a large plant and many posters of relief work hung on the wall. On the wall to the left of Zéni hung a brown bulletin board with all kinds of cards, many with thank you on them but also some just with pictures of families.

'Beautiful isn't it?" sounded a voice behind her. 'All inmates that I have been able to help personally and I can proudly say that these have all improved their lives, maybe one day you will be here.'

She turned and looked into the greenest eyes she had ever seen. It was exactly as if she were looking into a meadow, and all aggressiveness fell from her shoulders.

'Sit down, Mrs. Valler.'

Zéni sat down on the edge of her seat, and those green eyes had seen that immediately.

'Just relax, there are no men here who want to touch your breasts or put you in isolation.'

"So you saw that?

'There is little I don't see. That's why I told them to leave you alone, it was self-defense. And that you took a step closer yourself we'll forget,' she added with a smile.

"Well, thank you.

'No thanks, sometimes you have to show those men that women run the world.'

Zéni began to laugh; she thought that way too, she had to confess.

'So Zéni, how are you?'

'Not good, I'm stuck.'

'Yes, I understand that, but I take it you are well taken care of?'

"What do you mean?

'Aaa... no nothing, I just thought you had already made contact with some people? You've already called, I hope?'

"Who should I call?

'Nay, never mind, Mrs. Valler, I am probably wrong. Can happen huh, with so many inmates. I see our friend is being taken back to his cell, just go to the doctor and then back to your cell huh.'

Zéni got up looked at the director for a moment and then walked out the door. When she looked back for a moment, the director was busy on the phone, and from the way she was acting, it was an important call.

She quickly forgot about the conversation with the director and walked into the doctor's office.

'Can't you knock ... ow Mrs. Valler it's you, yes the director already said you were coming.'

Zéni looked around; the doctor's office was small. A desk in front of her with an old computer and an even older man behind it. Behind her there was a gurney and to her right a scale. There were all medical posters hanging on the wall here and the door behind the desk led to a pharmacy.

'Just walk through the door to your left.'

She looked to her left and saw a door she had not seen, walked through it and was momentarily surprised. This room was more like a storage area than something you'd expect to find at a doctor's office.

The walls were gray and there was a musty smell, boxes were piled everywhere and in the middle were more filing cabinets.

'Yes, just walk further back if you like?

She walked through and saw a large machine. She saw a black plate raised vertically.

'Stand with your chest against the plate please. Good stretch if you like and stay like that.'

She did as asked and stood her ground.

'Yes good, that's all right, now go back to your cell.'

'Huh, was that all?

'Yes, pictures have now been taken of your lungs, if all is well you won't hear anything.'

She walked away to the door and came back into the doctor's waiting room. What was immediately noticeable was that all the hallways were empty, and three agents were watching her through the fishbowl.

She walked up the stairs to the grille door on the highest floor and waited for someone to open it.

After a few minutes of waiting, an agent came and opened the bars and followed her up the stairs.

'I heard you've already had fun downstairs?'

'I was just defending myself; that man wanted to assault me.'

'That's what I've heard, yes. But I wouldn't spread it around too much if I were you, many women have connections with the men downstairs and we wouldn't want anything to happen, would we?

Zéni could only agree, the sooner she was out of here the better. When she was back in her cell, she was glad that was all behind her.

' You've been gone a long time?'

'Yes, there was all kinds of stuff going on downstairs.'

'Those men didn't bother you I hope? I never liked the idea of those roaming free when we have to go downstairs. Those beasts are shy for nothing.'

"No friends downstairs? Zéni asked very carefully because after what the officer said about having connections downstairs, pissing off her cellmate was the last thing she wanted.

'Friends? Down here? No. I once patted one on the face who sat on my butt when visiting.'

'Well, I've had the same thing,' Zéni said with relief and she told her story, only leaving out the case with the principal. She didn't want people to think she was getting preferential treatment.

'And you don't have to go to isolation? When I whacked that guy I managed to sit for a week. What did you do, suck the jailer?'

'I really don't know, I just know I'm lucky.'

They went on like this for a while, until the jailer came with dinner and a ticket for Zéni. It was a red ticket with two codes on it.

"That's your phone code, with it you can see on that phone how much credit you have and how much money is in your account.'

"Then I don't need that, I don't need to call, and I don't know who's depositing me money.'

'Still, you should activate that sometime, they're hard on you if you don't. The trouble they put in for you and stuff,' Amy said as she poked at her dinner that Zéni had passed by, she wasn't hungry anyway.

She looked at the card for a moment and then picked up the receiver of the phone. "*Please enter your personal code,*" the female voice said into the phone. She looked at the card again and then typed in "26843629." "*Enter your personal PIN next.*" "3546".

"*To change your pin, enter four numbers and close with the hashtag key.* She thought for a moment and then typed 7525, it was a number she had in her head since childhood, only she didn't know where she knew that combination from.

'*Your current phone balance is €0.00. Your current prison account balance is €100.00.*'

"Prison account balance, what is that?" asked Zéni uncertainly.

'That's the money in your account to order things from the canteen list.'

'And does everyone get 100 euros?'

'WHAT, no, absolutely not. Do you already have money? You just got here. Usually it takes four days.'

'I don't know who it came from, I don't have anyone outside.'

"From your parents?

'Nay... that's impossible. She became silent for a moment. 'Who can send me money? I don't have anyone.'

'Well, you can write a report bill to BDW, there you can ask for a statement of account. The sender's name must be on it, right?'

Lacking any other ideas, Zéni wrote a letter to BDW, only she had to wait until tomorrow night before she could deliver it.

In the evening, Amy fell asleep immediately. Zéni kept turning and wondering who had sent her money. Surely she knew she had no one. Her mother had died and her father had bailed. After hours she saw the sun rise and even then it took her a while to catch sleep. When she woke up again she was in pain all over her body and they had already been for lunch which she had missed.

Before she knew it, it was evening and she was able to hand over the bill; now she had to wait for an answer.

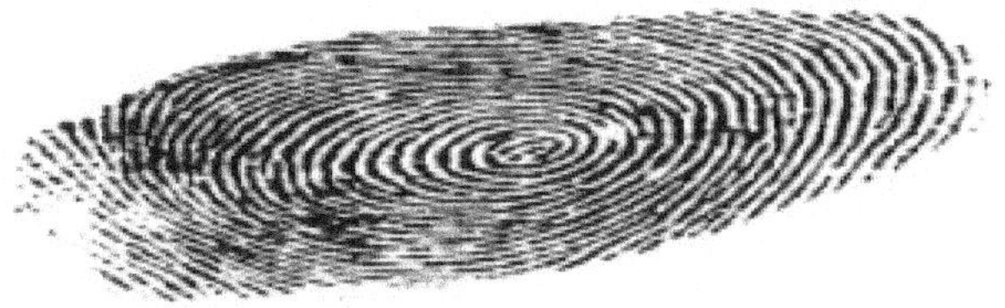

Chapter 4

When Zéni woke up, Amy was already busy receiving the coffee and soup.

'Mail has been brought for you.' She handed Zéni the piece of paper her request was stapled to. She removed the bill from it and looked at the larger paper.

"Account statement Zéni Valler" it said. It said what her available amount was and also whether anything had been set aside to go out of the account, but this did not interest her: she just wanted to know who had deposited the money so she looked further and there she saw it.

"10/02/20 deposited by: Unknown, amount deposited: €100,

11/02/20 deposited by: Unknown, amount deposited: €100."

Like a man possessed, she ran to the phone and typed in the two codes. '*Your current phone balance is €0.00. Your current prison account balance is €200.00,*' said the female voice on the line.

She hooked the phone and looked at Amy. 'There's €200 on it already.'

'Don't question it too much, be glad you have something. There are many sitting here with no money. Take the list and order something now.'

She picked up the list and looked at it, actually Amy was right: it wasn't worth having nothing of "luxury" here just because she wanted to know who the money belonged to. She had better things to do herself than wonder about that, she thought.

So she ordered all sorts of things from the list that she could use and suddenly for Amy as well because she saw that she only ordered a few things herself and always when she went to the phone she turned the sound down to the quietest setting and turned the receiver away.

'How much money do you actually have?

"That doesn't matter, and you don't have to order anything for me. I've seen it.

Zéni looked at her out of the corner of her eye and crossed her arms. 'I just order what I want and if I want to share you just have to let me,' she said with a smile in her voice. 'And now you're going to say how much you have or I'll steal your codes and check it myself.'

'Okay, I currently have €11, and when I've ordered this €6.'

"Thank you for saying it, see, I apparently have a secret admirer who knows I'm here so we'll use this together, understand?

"How does such a good person end up in prison here?" said Amy with tears in her eyes and she hugged Zéni.

'It's all right. If I used everything by myself I would feel guilty anyway so I just can't do anything else.'

"Am I interrupting an intimate moment here or can I join in?" suddenly sounded a voice behind the two. They looked back and saw an officer in the doorway.

'Letter for Valler and you may suddenly sign for receipt.'

"What is this?

'Your letter that you have to appear Friday. Now, it's on strike, so you're probably not going to be able to go there yourself, but your lawyer is going to be there.'

She walked to the door, signed the paper, got another one handed to her and walked back to the table where she read through it briefly.

'It doesn't say much anyway, just that my business is at nine in the morning.'

'Yes, a lot of text without meaning, so are a lot of papers here."

The hours and days that followed intertwined. They spent time talking, watching TV or sleeping. That was all there was to do anyway, and before they knew it, it was Friday morning.

From that morning it was clear that Zéni was being treated differently from the rest of the inmates, and Amy also began to catch on. The officers came in every hour to report on her case and she also once got her lawyer on the line via cell phone. She didn't know much to say but the act said more than words could.

'What's going on here, Zéni?" asked Amy as a cop walked away with the cell phone. 'Nobody gets to hold a cell phone in here without bribing a cop, and they offered it themselves?'

In the few days they sat together, Amy had become more and more of a friend, and she couldn't keep lying to her, so she told everything that had happened at the principal's office.

'So the director hinted that you needed to call someone? And afterwards there was €200 in your account? Quite a coincidence huh?

To be perfectly honest, Zéni had not looked at it that way but it was quite a coincidence not to be linked she thought. "Yes now that you mention it, I hadn't thought about it.

'Do you know how to verify that if you are being pulled ahead?' She looked at Zéni with big eyes full of expectation when the latter answered nothing. 'Ask the chief here if you can go directly to the director, if they allow it you will get everything done here. If not it's a coincidence.'

She had to think about that for a moment, it was common knowledge that to get to the director you could wait days so if she could get to it right now what Amy said was true. On the other hand, she didn't know if she wanted to know.

'Mrs. Valler, director wants to see you.'

There went the chance to test it, they both realized. Zéni joined them, again all the way down the hallway, and again they noticed that the hallways were empty.

Once she arrived at the director's office, she immediately sat back down in the chair without waiting for an invitation, and not to her surprise, she did nothing.

'Zéni, I regret to inform you that you have been extended for one month. You will therefore be taken to a cell suitable for a longer stay because where you are now is only for the first few days in observation.'

'Are you giving everyone this notice personally or is it just with me?'

For a moment there was silence and it seemed as if she was seeing how far she could go with answers.

'There's not that many men today being extended, I'd rather do it myself.'

Somehow she didn't believe anything that was said but still she nodded understandingly and thanked her.

'I do want to ask, since we find that things are going exactly right between you and your cellmate, whether you would like to take them into your next cell with you, or would you rather not?'

'Yes, Amy is a good person.'

'Okay, I'll see what I can do.'

They remained looking into each other's eyes for a moment, and then the director handed Zéni a stack of papers in her hand. 'Here are your arrest papers for a month.' Then she stood up and pointed Zéni to the door. An officer was already standing there to take her upstairs.

When she stood back in the cell, everything was packed and Amy stood in the middle of the room.

'The cops just came to tell us to pack everything, they're going to split us up.' The crying was closer to her than the laughter.

'No, they're not going to do that. The director has asked if I want you in my next cell and of course I said yes.'

Again Amy flew into Zéni's arms for a big hug and she gave one back. Here was a friendship made for life.

After a while, an officer came to get the two women and took them to another wing, on the other side of the fishbowl. Farthest away from the stairs in the hallway.

When they were past the grille door of this wing she saw that it consisted of two floors, there was a staircase without a railing in the middle of the corridor. They walked to the first cell door and the officer opened it.

The two walked inside where they were stared at by six pairs of eyes. As they walked in, Zéni saw that fortunately this cell was larger than the one for two. There was a separate room for the toilet immediately to the right and next to that door hung the telephone, which meant that to have some privacy you could make a call in the toilet.

Behind the corner of the toilet, she saw two sinks that, like in the other cell, had shelves and mirrors. She just remembered that she had not looked in the mirror for five days and resolved to do so as soon as possible.

Next to the sinks were two bunk beds that stood back to back against the wall where there were two windows and a television set hung between them. Under the TV was a small refrigerator, opposite it she saw three similar cupboards as downstairs, and immediately she knew that this was too little for eight men.

To her left, she saw a table with cutlery, plates and bowls. Also on it was a shelf with boxes full of butter, sugar and jam. Then next to the table were two bunk beds again up to the cabinets she just saw. In the middle of the room were two tables with four chairs at each.

"Welcome to our clubhouse," said the woman sitting on the bed downstairs next to the sink. She was old with short gray hair and had a face that had a surprising amount of humor on it. 'The bed above me and then the bed behind it is still free,' she said pointing to the bed above her and the one next to it.

'Perfect, thanks,' Amy and Zéni said together as they walked to the designated beds and put their things there. They would cover the bed later, they thought.

Zéni turned to the woman who pointed out the beds to her and held out her hand. "Good day, my name is Zéni.

"My name is Georgette.

She turned to the rest and went to the woman closest to her, it was a slightly chubby woman with long, thin, black hair and a hook nose who introduced herself as Nicol. Next to her stood a tall sturdy woman with blonde hair cut into bangs and firm cheekbones that gave her a stern face, she introduced herself as Jennifer and spoke with a distinctly Dutch accent.

On the other side of the room stood three more women, the first in line had brown hair down to her rear, was tinted in color and had very small brown eyes, she called herself Laura. Next to them stood two the same in appearance: both medium length blonde hair, a beautifully shaped little face and deep blue eyes, the brightest blue you ever saw. Clearly Swedish twins, their names were Ira and Ela.

When they had both become acquainted with everyone, Zéni sat down on her bed and began to get to know the women a little better.

"And what facts are you here for?" asked the woman who called herself Georgette.

'I'm here for dealing narcotics,' Zéni said bluntly.

'I'm in for burglaries,' Amy said after some hesitation, it was clear she didn't feel right having to say this in front of such a large group, as if she had broken into one of theirs. Which of course was real, after a while you've had every house.

"And found much, Amy?

'Way too much,' she said briefly, showing that she did not want to go into it further, which Georgette understood and respected.

"What about you guys?" asked Amy who sensed tension in the group.

'I sit for discharging chemical waste in public,' Georgette said.

'Wow, is there a lot of money to be made from that?'

'If you're smart about it, yes, chemical waste disposal legally costs a lot so if you can make it disappear you can grab money.'

'I'm in for dealing drugs in Belgium but as you hear I'm from the Netherlands,' Jennifer said. 'Less punishment in the Netherlands, just more money to be made in Belgium,' she added with a smile.

'I'm sitting for an argument with my husband, nothing bad really but the neighbors called the police, they wanted to take my husband away and I then intervened. We're both sitting here.' That was Nicol.

'We're here for drugs too, like most here in Antwerp.' That was Ira from the twins. 'We were making contacts because nothing can grow at our place in Sweden. We were just at a supplier for quality when they raided. The men were able to escape, we were caught. With that last she pointed at her and her sister and then shrugged.

'Now they certainly hope you'll click.'

'Yes, so we sit here for a while because we don't say anything'

'It's already a surprise that you get to sit together in one cell.'

'Yes we were able to arrange that because we are sisters in a foreign country, you have easy rules if you know them.'

'Yes with me too drugs, especially Ketamine and xtc. ' That was Laura. 'Robbed my friend and he said it was mine.'

'Wow, and that from your friend.'

'Yes, but I should have expected it, he already had a criminal record and I don't so it's less time spent sitting for me.'

That was true, Zéni thought, but still she thought the friend should be allowed to take responsibility. She didn't say that out loud, of course, but when she exchanged a glance with Amy, she knew she felt the same way.

Zéni then decided to make her bed and load her closet; she had been given one shelf from the closet and had to make do with it. The closet was far too small for eight women.

When everything was over, it was already time for dinner. Sandwiches with tuna salad. When they sat down at the table, Laura, Georgette and Ira got up and walked to their cupboard or refrigerator.

"Anyone have a Coke?" asked Laura, looking especially at Amy and Zéni because they hadn't gotten stuff from canteen yet.

'That would actually be kind if you can spare one, we'll give that back to you as soon as possible.'

"That's not how we work here. That was Georgette returning with a box of hard-boiled eggs. 'If we have something we share, we also see what we order with all of us. Then we have something for everyone and are never short. If you want an egg grab it, hey ladies.' And with the last said, she passed the box around.

'Well, then I would like a Coke and an egg,' Zéni said, and she was immensely happy to have ended up in this cell along with human women.

When dinner was finished and everyone had placed their plates in the sink, most of the ladies remained at the table.

"Shall we do the dishes then, Zéni?" asked Amy who was already standing up. Zéni also stood upright and joined in.

'Thank you ladies, that's tremendously kind of you,' Nicol said and the rest nodded approvingly.

After the dishes were washed, the table was cleared by Ira and Ela and everyone lay down on their beds to watch the news. When that was done a movie was put on and chips, nuts and drinks were passed around.

And for the first time, Zéni felt at ease and realized how stressed she had been the last few days and how blessed she was to be in the cell first with Amy and now with the rest. And for a moment she forgot the case of the unknown money lender.

The next day, Zéni woke up after a first quiet night, which she found strange because it was the first time she had slept with so many people in one room.

When she turned and looked around she saw Georgette standing at the door, accepting jugs, and Laura was putting the soup on the table. 'Good morning Zéni,' she said when she saw that one was awake. 'Slept well I hope?'

'Well, could be better I must confess. Can I help you?

"Yes, if you could just take the bread from the table at the door and put it on the dining table, please?

When everything was ready, eight of them attacked and there was silence. The onion soup was simple but delicious and together with the coffee it seemed exactly like they were eating at an inn among friends. There was laughter and conversation as if they had known each other for years.

When the food was finished and everything cleaned up everyone went about the day in their own way. Ira and Ela were talking in Swedish on one of their beds. Laura was playing cards with Georgette and Nicol and Jennifer was reading a book.

Amy had gone to bed for a while and Zéni decided to watch the game of cards then: maybe she was learning another new card game.

After watching for a while she thought she had figured it out, each player had an equal number of cards (depending on the number of players) and you had to take turns throwing a card on the table with the signs down and saying what you were throwing, the opposing player then had to guess whether you were lying or not. If the player thought you were lying then he could take the card. If she was right you got the card back, if not she had to take it herself.

If the player thought you were right he could also throw up one more and so the game continued. Because of these rules, Zéni had already seen a few times when for three rounds they said there was a 2 on the table even though there were 9 cards on the table.

When Laura took the card and hoped to see through the lie, she saw that Nicol's last card was indeed a 2 and so she had to take the whole pile herself.

It was a game of lying and bluffing and she liked that and the other two were doing well too.

After a while, the door opened and they heard the officer call in. "Canteen operation!

The ladies left everything as it was and hurried to the door to take on the canteen.

When it was finally Zéni's turn and the whole load of colas, candy and other products for care, she thought again of her anonymous backer, and it had occurred to the rest as well when all her products were on the bed.

"Wow girl, where did you get your *sugardaddy*?" asked Ira, and she saw the rest looking interested.

'That's a good question, when I came in here a reasonable amount of money had been deposited by an unknown person.' They would find out anyway, in a room of eight you don't really keep anything secret.

'What do you mean unknown? Surely you can get a transcript from BDW, and it does have to have every name on it that you send something. That's mandatory.

'Yes, I thought so too, and I applied for that one too.' And she showed the printout of her bill.

Hours were spent speculating who the money came from, finally when it was well into the evening and they couldn't think of an answer they all went to sleep.

The next morning they woke up earlier than usual and for a moment Zéni thought something bad was going on, so she jumped out of bed in just her underwear and stood looking around. Everyone looked at her with an amused expression.

'Well, if you want to shower first, you can go,' Laura said.

'Huh, showering, is that now?'

'Yes sleepyhead, every other day outside on weekends like always.'

Zéni looked at the bed where Amy was sleeping and realized that she too had not showered in a while.

'Okay, thank you, are you sure I can go first?'

'Yes, you're ready anyway. Put something on first, though, because they don't like you standing like that.'

She looked down and saw that she was standing in the middle of the room in her underwear. She didn't care much, after all she had a body to show for it, nevertheless she put on a pair of pants and T-shirt anyway. Grabbed her towel and shampoo and walked out the door.

In the hallway, she didn't know where to go. Every door she saw looked like a cell, and nowhere was there a sign saying shower.

"First time showering in this hallway?" said a voice behind her that seemed to come from an officer.

When she said nothing, she pointed to a door on the right side of the hallway. "That's where the shower is.

'Thank you,' Zéni said and she walked to the door, inside she saw three stalls with half doors with no lock.

She stepped inside and closed the door, which was so low you could see over it. To her luck, the shower itself was in the back of the stall and was covered by another wall.

She undressed and turned on the shower. The drizzle that came out was not much and the water was lukewarm, yet she enjoyed it as if she had never had a shower before and was already relieved that it was not like showering together like on television. How wrong the movies and series on television were, she thought to herself.

She washed off all the dirt and stress from her body and thought about how she had felt the past few days, mostly indifferent and somewhere she was not surprised. All her life she had been struggling and surviving and somewhere this was no different, only that anonymous moneylender she found caring because she didn't like being in debt to anyone and especially if she didn't know to whom.

After the shower she dried off and dressed again, like a reborn she walked to the cell door and waited for an officer to open it. She walked inside and put her towels on the heater to dry, when she walked to her bed there was an envelope on it with her name: *"Zéni Valler cell 2231"*.

"When was this brought?

'Just now, when you were showering. Why? Is something wrong?

"Not at all, I was just wondering if I had been lying on it," she lied.

She grabbed the letter and turned it over to see who the sender was. No sender written on it.

'Normally when a letter is sent, shouldn't there be a sender on it in case the letter has to be returned?'

'Normally yes, but they open them here and sometimes they put them in a new envelope.'

All the relaxation from a moment ago was gone and it felt like her shoulders were stuck again.

She opened the envelope and reread the letter, each letter she read adding a quirk to her forehead. So many that it hurt.

"Zéni Valler,

You probably don't know me and that makes sense.

I assume you have already seen that €200 has been deposited into your prison account, I understand you want to know who it came from.

Call at 8 p.m. tonight at the number: 0487543296"

She read through the letter three or four times and still didn't get it. She looked at the clock and saw that it was only seven o'clock. Time for coffee and soup.

The day passed slowly. She tried to spend her day playing games and watching movies. When it was finally eight o'clock she sprinted to the phone, dialed the number and stood in the bathroom, afraid of what was coming and curious to know who she was going to hear.

The phone rang and rang, and it took a long time for someone to answer at the other end.

"Hello?" sounded a deep voice on the other end of the line.

'Hello, Dad,' Zéni said.

'Great, you already know who I am and you haven't hung up yet, this is going great.'

"What do you want?

'I want to talk to you. Bad that I have to pay 200 euros first but yes, better that than nothing right? How is it there?

'Yeah, that's not how we're going to do it, man. After years of not hearing anything we're going to deposit money and suddenly ask how it's here. Visiting can't be done for sure?'

'Yes, you have to request that if you want to, just fill out a paper and I'll be right there.'

'Gosh. My father following those rules. What is it? Don't you have a long arm anymore or something?'

"Sure you want to test that, Zéni?

'Yes, father, yes, you've never been there and now I'm going to have to fill out a piece of paper to see you. Come huh, make a little effort if you really want to see me.'

BEEP, BEEP, BEEP. The line was disconnected and Zéni stood in the toilet with the phone in her hands and shaking on her legs.

"Zéni Valler?" sounded on the other side of the door. She stepped out of the bathroom and hung the phone on the receiver.

'Come along,' said the broad cop in the doorway. He was at least six feet tall with a full head of hair and a long viking beard. What stood out most was that he had a black spot on his left ring finger as if a ring had been tattooed there.

"Where are we going?

'No questions asked, Valler. Just come with me, you'll be right back.'

She raised her shoulders and walked along to the hallway. Through the grille door and down the stairs again. The hallways were empty again which didn't surprise her this time because it was late and everyone was in front of the television watching a movie.

All the way down, the agent walked to the fishbowl in the middle where an agent was looking bored at the screens. Once she reached the speaker, she heard a BIEP, and spoke to the agent who had taken her.

'Valler, Zéni, video call.'

'Okay, let her walk on.'

"Come with me.

They walked on the right side of the fishbowl past the doctor's waiting room and the director's office that was now empty. There was a glass door behind which she could see the corridor, which she recognized as the one she had entered.

A soft buzz let out that the door was loose, the officer opened it, let Zéni through and without looking up at her said, "Enter third door on the right.

She walked through the door and passed two doors that were both closed and the light was off, at the third she saw it open and the light on. She went in, closed the door and it went straight into the lock.

Inside, she saw a table with a single chair in front and, on the other side of the table, a large television screen with a blue screen on it.

She sat down and the screen jumped on. There on the other side of the screen sat a man of what Zéni thought must be in his forties now. His dark brown hair lay combed back with a parting on the left side and his thin beard was nicely trimmed and perfectly lined. His eyes bright blue and firm jaws.

'Bye Dad, it's not what I thought but I'm still shocked to see you here.'

"You see, daughter, I still have a long arm.

'Yes, apparently. Now I've seen you so I'm going back to my cell.' She got up and wanted to walk to the door, which was still locked.

'No Zéni you are going to have to listen to me for a while. I have never been a good father but you must understand that if I stayed with you it was not going to be safe for you. I have made many enemies over the years and they would not stop pursuing us.'

'So now all of a sudden you can contact me? Now you're not afraid of people or what would happen to me?'

'What was there then is resolved, Zéni, I understand that you are not happy to see me but I am making all this effort to hear you now that you are in need. I want to help you get outside so we can build something together.'

'I don't want to be helped by you, I'm staying here until the judge decides otherwise, keep out of this. If you still want to help send some money, that's all you're good for.'

She got up and walked to the door, which was now open. As she stood in the doorway she turned once more to the television and she saw her father looking at someone behind the camera. When he saw her watching he still said, "Sometimes we don't have a choice what to do, princess, I'll see you around. And with a wink, a blue screen came on the television and the conversation was over.

She walked to the hallway where an officer was waiting at the metal detector, she walked through it and when it didn't go off she sat down in the waiting room in front of the BAD, contemplating everything.

So her father had found out she was stuck, suddenly wanted to reconnect and make everything right and wanted to help her out of this? And what was that at the end: "Sometimes we don't have a choice what to do, princess, I'll see you around. " Never before had anyone called her princess.

Once back upstairs in her cell, everyone was ready to hear her story, and even though she hadn't known the rest of the cell very long, she felt she could trust them. And she had to tell someone, who knows, maybe the girls would have a different take on it.

After again speculating for hours, no one could put a rope to it and they all went to sleep one by one.

Days passed and nothing indicated that she would see her father again. Everything was quiet and she had almost forgotten about the confrontation with him. Thinking about everything she had to arrange for her lawyer and worrying about the verdict of the trial soon.

When Zéni and Amy were in jail for two weeks, Laura had to appear, and when she returned in the afternoon, the smile on her face was so big that it split her face in two.

'I get to go home! I can go home!" she cried, rather redundantly, judging by her smile and the fact that she was jumping a hole in the air.

"Great!" cried Georgette.

'Oooh, I love this so much for you,' Amy said and the rest of the day was spent celebrating and drinking and snacking.

When they came to get Laura in the evening and closed the door behind her the cell became silent, everyone crawled back into their beds and even the television was off. Everyone was happy for Laura but also realized that it meant there was a new one at the door tomorrow and you never know who it would be and what her character would be like.

After a very restless night, Zéni got up while everyone else was still sleeping. She looked up at the door and saw that there was an envelope on the floor.

She walked to the door and was not surprised to see her own name on it. When she opened the envelope she was so shocked that she dropped it and stood there with trembling hands.

Inside the envelope was a photograph of her father, tied to a chair, blood running from the corners of his mouth and from a wound on his head. He looked bad. His hair and beard still looked the same as in the video call they had had but his gray T-shirt had been pulled out so far that the neckline hung down on his chest and one of his sleeves had been torn off.

When she picked up the picture again, she noticed there was a letter behind it.

"Zéni Valler,
What your father said about people coming after him was not a lie.
Now, regretfully for him and you, he cannot fulfill his part of the bargain
and must pay.
Look what you did when you rejected your father "princess." If you ever
want to see your father again, make sure you get out of your hotel there. I
know you can do it but remember: your father has a long arm and your
good relationship with the director is not going to help you.
When you are outside go to the park in Schoten, there you will further get
your assignment."

She read through the letter three times and then burned it, some things must remain secret. When she had flushed away the ashes in the toilet and burned away the smell by burning an orange peel, she went back to the living area of the cell where everyone was still sleeping and walked to the window, the first time she looked outside.

Their cell overlooked a square with a painted wall across the street. In the plaza was a soccer field, a canopy and there were a few fitness machines placed walled in by a wall that was as high as the six-story prison, so once atop the roof you already didn't have to worry about jumps to do. Now to get on the roof.

On the wall that ran perpendicular to theirs, she also saw a light pole hanging from the wall next to each window, if she could get the grating off the window she might be able to climb up through the light pole.

Of course then she had to be able to grind through metal and do so without her cellmates hearing, she could forget that, she thought.

Still, she decided to remember that path and go outside with her on the next walk to get a better look at everything.

She lay back in bed and waited patiently for the first to wake up, as always it was first Georgette who, because of her back, could never sleep long. Gradually the rest woke up and Zéni also crawled out of bed.

Breakfast came and went again, bland carrot soup with lukewarm coffee. She was tired of that food here, too, and secretly she was already thinking about the food she would eat when she was outside, which would have to wait.

Around three o'clock in the afternoon when even the midday meal had long passed, this time spaghetti bolognese which was surprisingly very good, the officer came to ask who was going for a walk and for the first time Zéni stood up and reported that she wanted to walk.

'Oooh are you going for a walk, Zéni? Then I'll come along I think, I've always wanted to see where the walk is.' That was Amy and Zéni looked up at her worriedly upon hearing that the walk would not be in this square.

'That's the square here if you look outside, isn't it?'

'Nay, this square here belongs to the working men. Haven't you ever stood and watched them play sports? You should definitely do it sometime, sometimes it's worth it.'

Talking further about the men she had seen sporting the broad arms, Amy dressed to go outside with them. Zéni was already not listening; all she thought was that she could forget her plan.

When the agent came to get them, the hall was full, at each door there were at least two agents. When they got outside, Zéni and Amy had to turn around and were searched by an officer, then they were directed to a door about halfway down the hallway that led into a stairwell.

Going down the stairs, Zéni could already see part of the square through the small windows placed on each floor.

The square looked about the same as the one their cell looked onto only here there was no painted wall, but the walls were the same length. One problem: their cell was on the other side. Maybe if she could go over the roof?

When they got outside she enjoyed her first rays of sunshine on her face. It was now late February and surprisingly good weather for the time of year. The sun was shining full on the square making it tremendously warm and the occasional cool breeze provided just enough refreshment.

She walked around the square for a moment, enjoying the space she had to walk, it felt like she was reborn, like she had never walked before.

She walked and walked and walked, it was in circles but still it seemed like she was walking across a green meadow. The sun on her face and the wind at her back. For a moment she forgot all her worries and was taken back to a better time. A time she had never remembered until now.

She was a little girl and was walking by the hand of a man by the side of a river or a canal. They stopped and fed the ducks with bread they had brought, she looked aside at the man and saw a bloodied face. Blood was running from the corners of his mouth and from his eyes; there was dried blood on his forehead.

She woke up from her thoughts and looked up. I am in prison, what I just saw was a play of my mind just because I felt sun and wind. How weak can I be.

For a moment she had to search until she found Amy again, who was still standing at the level of the door and looking up at the wall.

"What are we looking at?

Amy was startled when Zéni stood behind her and spoke the words, for a moment she looked like she had been caught like a child stealing candy behind her mother's back.

'Nothing you know, I was just seeing how it was built here. I never saw how the construction was so I'm a little disoriented and I'm not used to that.'

'Or, like a good thief, you are not only looking for ways in but also ways out,' she said with a laugh in her voice, but a plan also came into her brain. A thief always had a way in but also a way out. 'How would you go about it, do you think? I was thinking if you get rid of the grating in front of the windows that you could climb up to the roof and then get out? She tried to make it sound as casual as possible, but she still saw Amy looking suspicious. 'Well, you're not the only one who's broken into a house before, I'm looking at ways out, too.'

"That's a story I'd like to hear. There was a hint of empathy as an undertone.

'Well, if you say what you think, I'll tell my story.'

She saw Amy thinking for a moment and was just about to say forget it, and just tell the story of the one time she had broken into her ex's house, when she saw that Amy was not looking at her, but at the wall.

'Well, the wall is not to be done, there are far too many cameras. If you can already climb the wall like a spider you'll be caught in no time.'

'And if you wear black? In the middle of the night?

Amy did look at her now, as if she had said something funny. 'Either you've never stayed awake past midnight, or you're not paying attention.'

'I have better things to do than look outside in the middle of the night.'

'Yes and now suddenly you want to know all about it and you are watching. What's going on, Zéni?

'Nothing, see, if you don't want to say your reservations we'll leave it that way and go play sports.'

She let the words sink in for a moment and already began walking silently toward the fitness machines set up farther away.

'Okay, we'll make a deal, girl.'

Zéni turned as if stung. Perhaps a little too quickly because Amy hesitated a little again, but then pressed on anyway.

'You tell your story, and you say what you're up to. And don't say nothing,' she added when she saw that Zéni wanted to protest again. 'So your story of breaking in, what you plan to do, and then I tell you what I think, right?'

Zéni didn't have to think about that and so she agreed almost immediately, hesitating only to keep up appearances.

'So the walls are out of the question. Even if you wear black and climb in the middle of the night, first of all you already have to get through the grating, and with eight in the cell that's not going to happen. Then if you get through at all there are always lights burning outside, aimed at the wall so black doesn't make much difference.'

She stopped for a moment and looked at Zéni, who had to admit that it was very optimistically conceived, and fairly amateurish.

'Let's walk around, if we stand too long looking at the walls we'll get noticed.'

She had to agree with Amy on that too. There was more to her than Zéni had first thought. "So there's actually no way to get outside? The desperation was almost impossible to miss in Zéni's voice; she didn't really want to keep up appearances for Amy anymore anyway.

'Through the window and over the wall you can actually forget, yes. But how old is this prison?'

She surprised Zéni with that, how was she supposed to know how old this building was? And what did it matter? It remained silent and Zéni looked at Amy uncomprehendingly.

'Well, this prison has been in service for about a hundred and sixty years, I think,' Amy finally said. 'I've done my research, Zéni, as you already know: a good burglar knows where she's going in, or well in my case: sitting.'

'Okay, all well and good but I don't suppose we can knock down the walls because of age?'

'Mrs. Valler, why are you so obsessed with the walls?'

'Those are the biggest obstacles you have to overcome, right?'

'What do you do when you can't cross an obstacle, neither around it nor through it?'

'God, you sound just like my math teacher back in the day when I couldn't solve a problem.' At this comparison, a broad smile came to Zéni's face; her math teacher couldn't be further from Amy. Her face resembled that of a fat toad and she strictly followed the rules, and did always manage to find the one who didn't. Which wasn't hard, because Zéni was always there.

'Well if you can't go over, beside or through you go under, right?' The way Amy said it, it just seemed like the most obvious thing to do.

'So you want to dig a tunnel on our sixth floor? Let me guess: we also use spoons like in the movies.' She was already beginning to regret asking for help; it was clear that Amy knew what she was talking about but didn't really bother to make a solid plan.

'No, or you must be able to do that then I want to look.'

After these words, Zéni became really angry, she was standing here wasting precious time while her father needed her. Strange, though, that after all these years of having no contact, she immediately wanted to escape because her father was in trouble.

Surely it was nothing new that her father had enemies; she had never known exactly what he did. But she did know that it was in the underworld, those who could not keep up with it were ruthlessly slaughtered. She had experienced it herself several times.

She angrily walked away from Amy and began peering down the walls again. Somewhere there had to be a weak link in it; it's in every structure, there was no other way. Maybe if she could make sure the lights were off, she could still climb.

'*End of the walk,* ' she heard a voice call through a speaker, and she saw the door open on the other side of the square.

Amy was waiting for her but she just walked through the door back upstairs.

Once inside the cell she left everyone for a moment and went to the bathroom, on the other side of the door she heard Amy say something about stomach upset from eating. The door opened and she joined Zéni.

'I'm glad you figured it out yourself.'

Zéni looked up in surprise and saw Amy smiling from ear to ear.

'Oh no, please don't say you just came here to sit for nothing. For here is your way to escape.'

Now she didn't understand, how could there be a road in such a small space? Surely there were no grates or windows to get through?

'The toilet pipeline has never been replaced, that is, they are still connected directly to the sewer here. And they're big enough for a grown man, it's been tested before.'

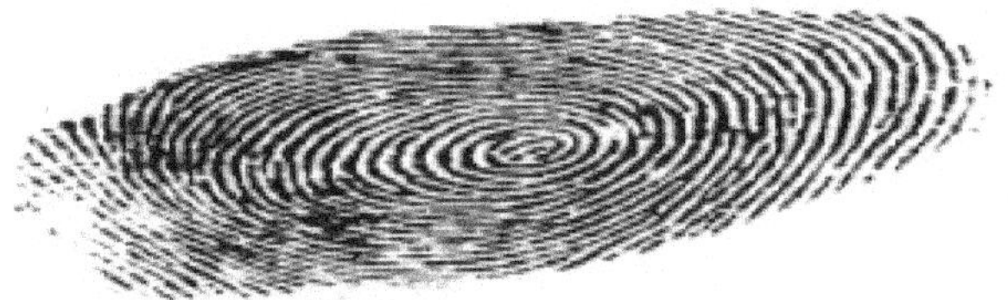

They were all sitting at the table. Amy had promised her that the story was still to come, only Georgette had to tell it because she knew the story better. Only to get it into the conversation without being noticed they had to wait a while.

So Zéni and Amy had come back from the restroom and had said that the food had taken a little to her stomach, but that she was better again.

Now they had just eaten and Amy had started talking about burglaries she had experienced and was telling a few stories about people she knew in prison. Whether they were all true Zéni doubted and it didn't matter. Amy was not only a good burglar but also a good storyteller.

'So they tied blankets together that they had kept aside from the laundry. Shot the light outside with a homemade slingshot and climbed to freedom," she concluded one of her stories.

'Too bad there are bars in front of this,' Laura said looking sadly at the window.

"Yes, it is," Amy said thoughtfully and then as if it just came to her mind she looked at Georgette and said, "But that's true girl, you told about an outbreak here this week, didn't you?

Georgette was surprised that the call had gone to her and had to think for a moment, but finally said, 'Yes, that's true, I had almost forgotten I told you. But everyone has heard that one, right?

'I didn't,' Zéni said. 'But now I'm curious.'

Amused, she watched Zéni, as much as Georgette often liked to stay in the background, she did enjoy having the rookies come to her for questions and stories. And this was an excellent story.

'A few years ago, nobody knows how long but it can't have been more than ten years. Two men who had committed a murder, something about the youngest's sister being harassed. Or was she harassing that man now no one knew and dared to ask. She stopped for a moment to drink from her glass, building the tension. 'So the two come in and think because it's about a sister they'll be out soon. Like always that nonsense "Mr. Judge my client only acted in defense of the female person who was harassed". So they have a bad judge and hear they both get twenty-five years, not really what they were hoping for.'

Again that silence, if only this time to let the number sink in. Twenty-five years is a tremendously long time, and no matter how old you are, you are not good for a while. Zéni thought about what she herself would do if she got twenty-five years and then decided to break out or end it. Whichever was easiest then.

'So the two men decide to break out, you know like normal people decide when they have their punishment. Now, what a lot of people don't know is that this is an old building, about a hundred and sixty-five years old. The pipeline here is so wide that a grown man can get through and he ends up right in the sewer.

Of course, to get there you have to dig out a section of adjacent pipes first and those are the shower and the toilet. From the shower you never dig so the only choice was the toilet, they dug for three months, removed the toilet and did their errands in the sink. What they did with the big message we don't know and I don't want to know. Again she stopped for a moment to drink and let everyone think about where the big message went.

'So in the night they took the toilet aside and started digging with tools they had from the kitchen and other places. Apparently the cement around the pipe is so cured that you can just scoop it out and you barely have to dig a few inches before you get to the widening. So a little digging and freedom was in sight. Now, this is just a story or rather a legend, the story is not real.'

'Well speaking of the toilet I really need to pee urgently girls" said Zéni as innocent as possible. "I'll be right back' She got up and walked to the toilet and Amy was the only one paying attention.

Once at the toilet, Zéni looked around the bottom of the toilet and picked a bit at the cement surrounding it, indeed, it came out very easily.

When she returned, she nodded unrecognizably to Amy, who returned a small smile.

When everyone was asleep, Zéni grabbed a spoon and once again tried to remove some cement. Surprisingly, it worked better than she ever expected, she removed cement piece by piece and soon saw a piece of pipe, the only thing that now bothered her was the toilet itself. To her luck, she had a thief on her side.

She went to sleep with immense satisfaction and slept as peacefully as sleep can be.

A few days passed, and Zéni and Amy had the tools to loosen the toilet: an old key they had found somewhere and a screwdriver to get rid of some more cement.

The hardest part was still getting the toilet out without the others noticing.

When there was a walk, Amy and Zéni were again the only ones from their cell outside and so they could discuss perfectly how they were going to handle it.

'So if we want to get away we have to move the toilet,' began Zéni

'Yes, not so fast girl, I said I was going to let my plans out after your story, now, I have already let my plans out. You didn't.'

She looked puzzled for a moment but realized that had indeed been the deal.

'So first the break-in and then why I want to leave here?'

'Doesn't matter in what order, as long as I hear them both.'

'My mother died at birth and my father left after that, which is basically the beginning of both stories. I was raised by foster parents and in care homes from the time I was born and from the age of 15 I ran away from everything. I wanted to look for my father or had a bad experience with the foster parents. Now, at one point I get to know a boy, Jens. I was seventeen at the time, he was eighteen, and he's the last person I ever let think I needed a man. He was a real bad boy, you know the ones, always stealing on the street and breaking and entering, and so on.

At one point the police are after me, it was the middle of the night and I had run away from my foster parents at the time. So police after me and I go to his home, I call on his cell phone and he doesn't answer. I then got into his yard, through the gutter on the porch and so to his window, where I saw him in bed with a blonde slut.'

She fell silent for a moment; even after all this time, it still hurt to talk about it and she had never actually told anyone, anyone.

'So I do the most logical thing: I break into his house by smashing the porch window with a stone from the garden, went upstairs, got the blonde out of bed and pushed him down the stairs and kicked him in the crotch. I was outside for two minutes when the police picked me up and by then they knew about the break-in.

"Is that why you don't let anyone near you?

'I just don't need a man who thinks I'm his plaything, it's why I went into the world of drugs. A woman gets more done than people think, I shake my ass once and men forget about quality and price, they pay anything I want.'

Amy looked at Zéni with wonder. "I absolutely understand you, now your latest story.

'This one is about my father, I have said he was not there at birth and left me to my own devices. Now recently I had a video conversation with him in which he said he had to because there were dangerous people after him who could make it dangerous for me. I thought it was all nonsense and excuses, but a few days ago I received a picture with my father tied up and with blood everywhere. The letter that came with it said I had to break out and save him. I know you probably think it's stupid, but I have to save him, abandoned or not.'

'I understand you completely, family always comes first no matter what, that's why I know what we're going to do.'

"*End of walk*. The conversation was held up by the speaker indicating the end of the walk. They went inside together and back to the cell.

Back inside, Zéni and Amy went their separate ways. Amy sat down on her bed and Zéni sat at the table and played a game of solitaire.

When it was evening and everyone was sitting in front of the television, Amy joined her on the bed, along with a notepad.

"*We need to make the toilet overflow, Zéni*," Amy wrote on the notepad and slid it toward her. She nodded, grabbed a pen and wrote back, "*Why and how?*"

Amy thought for a moment before writing and passing on the following: "*If the toilet is clogged the rest have no reason to go there, leaving us free.*"

It was not a bad plan Zéni had to admit, she nodded to Amy who got up and walked to the bathroom. She returned five minutes later with the smell of burnt orange peel and a puddle of water on the floor.

It took a few minutes for the rest to realize that water was running under the door and then a few more minutes for the whole game to get rolling. First it was Ira and then Georgette who saw the water running and after a while everyone was at the toilet door including the agents.

It was agreed that the toilet would not be used until the maintenance department had come by, everyone now had to go to the toilet in another empty cell and could not go again until tomorrow morning.

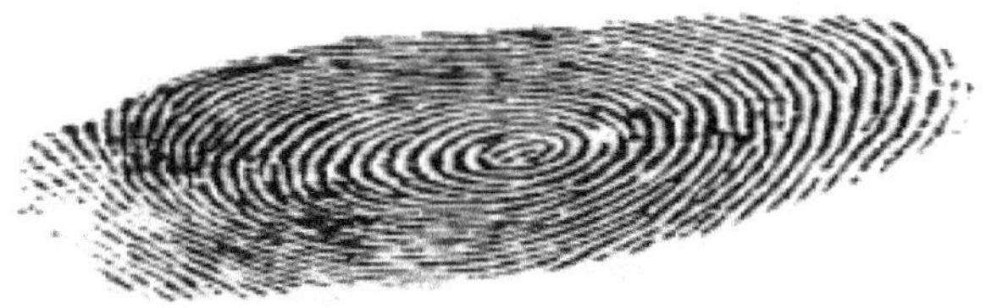

Chapter 6

When everyone was asleep Zéni and Amy went to the toilet door, they had brought matches to have light, towels to cover the crevices of the door and some more red sweaters they always had to put on when they went for walks in the square. They were spiteful sweaters but then they had some warmth.

They went inside and Amy began unscrewing the toilet while Zéni removed the cement with the screwdriver. After quite a while, the cement was gone and she saw part of the thicker pipe, which could certainly hold a grown man.

Amy finished unscrewing the toilet and lifted the toilet back a little, she saw to her happiness that the tubes were pushed together and not welded or glued. The thin tube had slid into the thicker part and they were able to get it out.

Only they had to make sure they didn't damage the connection for the water, that would have been a disaster and all of the toilet room and eventually the cell would have flooded.

Very carefully and precisely they lifted up the toilet, Zéni let her legs hang in the tube and felt no bottom which meant that at least the tube was going through.

'Now what if the tube downstairs gets thin again?' Amy looked very uncomfortably at the hole into which Zéni had stuck her legs.

Zéni looked at the hole and had to confess that she had thought of that too, but it was too late to turn back now and she would have to push through to save her father.

'If you want to follow me now is your chance, if you are afraid just go back to your bed.' And even before she could say anything or Zéni could change her mind, she turned away.

She used her hands and feet to gently slide herself down, the walls were wet and stank terribly. For a moment she thought she would suffocate from the gases separated by the excrement.

It was inhumanly dark below her and above her she heard nothing, she didn't know if Amy had jumped or not. She kept sliding and sliding, the stench and darkness were unbearable and when she thought it couldn't get any worse her right foot slipped.

Her shoulder came into hard contact with the tube and her nose was pushed into the excrement. She was sliding and vomiting at the same time. She was also falling and could not grasp anything due to the slippery walls.

The slope of the tube became less and less steep until she lay on her back in the excrement and had to crawl further on all fours, still the stench was one of the worst things but now she could also see several tubes coming out into her own tube.

The ground was full of poop and she heard water coming down behind her, someone had flushed and it was coming.

As fast as she could she crawled along, not realizing if she was making any progress or not. She made it through a few turns and noticed the tube getting bigger and bigger until she could finally stand straight there.

Here and there she saw a hole in the ceiling above her and saw that a small walkway had been made on either side of the river of excrement. She chose to walk on that and try to look through a hole.

She cringed when she saw a combi driving above her and for a moment she thought she had been caught, but the combi drove on and everything was fine.

She tried to see where she was but couldn't recognize anything and just walked on. Every so often she looked through a hole to see if she recognized anything. Finally she saw the KBC tower which meant she was at the Meir.

For a moment she continued walking until she saw some kind of alley she could get out of. Once at the top she had to take a moment to see where she was and cursed herself for not knowing the city better, the KBC tower was long gone and she didn't know the best way to get there.

Street in street out, but the tower she did not see. A little further on, she heard people coming and without thinking she put herself on the sidewalk against the wall with her head down, waiting for her victims.

They were a man and a woman of a wealthy nature. He had a nice black suit that by the looks of it cost quite a bit, she had a long red dress, high heels and lots of jewelry. Perfect, she thought.

The two had chosen the wrong alley; the couple walked by without looking back at Zéni. Only she could tell that the man turned his nose up at the scent she was spreading. When they had walked by, she stood up and grabbed the man by the back of his neck.

She bent down and turned at the same time so that he fell over her back to the ground, meanwhile she had already snapped the man's neck and focused on the woman before she could scream.

Zéni kicked at the inside of her kneecap which dislocated causing the woman to collapse and then gave her a knee to her temple.

When all that was done with extreme precision she put the couple aside and began to strip the woman of her clothes. In the handbag she found wet wipes and some makeup to make it look like she had only had a violent evening and not that she was from the sewer.

She also found three hundred and twenty-six euros worth of cash, an Audi brand car key and a ticket from Brabo parking garage.

Clumsy in heels and red dress, she walked out of the alley and looked back again to see if the couple was well hidden. Not for a moment did she feel any guilt toward the couple.

She walked out of the alley and saw the KBC tower on her left and stood in the middle of the Meir. She walked toward the tower, at the end of the Meir, where the street split into the egg market and the shoe market she grabbed the last of the two.

She walked on to where the bus was waiting and saw a large sign that said Brabo parking. She walked in and was glad it was the middle of the night that there was no one on the street. She did wonder what day it would be and wished she had remembered to look at a cell phone of the man or woman to see the day and time. But yes, nothing to be done about it, she thought philosophically.

She put her long brown hair in front of her eyes in case there were cameras and hoped she had a bit of a head start on the police who would probably have caught Amy. She felt very sorry for her because she had become attached to that silly girl, but as she told herself, family comes first.

She had to pass each car park to look for the car with the car's remote control. On the second floor, tucked between a KIA and a Volkswagen, was a gray Audi A5 sedan.

She opened the car, got in, started the car and looked around. The interior was covered in red leather with white stitching, in the center right of the steering wheel a screen had popped out as she started the engine. This screen now showed a map of Antwerp and the radio station 107.5, Radio Stad if she was correct.

The heels had to come off and it took a while to sucker in, she adjusted her seat and tore out of the parking lot at full throttle, the tires squealing across the floor, and she stopped further down the road with squealing tires at a pay machine.

She had to pay twenty euros, which to her luck was no problem, that couple had been a gift from heaven.

Once paid, she drove out of the parking lot, turned left into an alley that led to the quay. There she turned right toward the MAS, past Total gas station Bonaparte and toward the bridge to Merksem.

When she drove up there, she thought about it in time and turned the steering wheel to the left to continue driving next to the bridge and then through the Skyclub on the Albert Canal, because if she drove through the cinema there could be a huge amount of police.

She drove past the Skyclub, turned the corner and held her breath for a moment when she saw lights. An old green Opel Astra passed her without incident and she was able to continue driving.

She drove quietly but steadily on toward Schoten and in the meantime looked at the clock, it was ten hour in the night and it would take her ten to fifteen minutes to get to Schoten and then she had to find the safest way to the park.

She drove past the first few streets to Schoten and drove to the bridge she knew in Schoten as the bridge of "den breker" the dump place.

There she turned off, went down the bridge and drove out of Verbertstraat, came to the roundabout, took the third exit and drove into Jozef Hendrickxstraat. She drove out of that and turned left onto Kasteeldreef.

This street was known in Schoten for the beautiful lane with villas on both sides of the lane with trees every few meters and at the end of the street behind an arched gate the old castle of Schoten. Where the Count of Schoten had lived for many years and which was still a great sight as a Schotener.

She drove out of the lane and before the gate she turned down a side street to the parking lot. There she parked the car and turned off the engine.

She kept waiting and waiting there, the silence was murderous again and she felt fatigue fall over her now that she had escaped. She wondered if the police had already come after her and if anything had happened to Amy, she also thought for a moment about the couple she had had to kill and for a moment she regretted it.

She woke up and when she looked at the clock it was six in the morning, she looked around to see if she saw a new car yet but there was nothing in sight. She stretched and rested her hand on the passenger seat for a moment.

There, her hand touched something cold and metallic; she was startled and looked to the right. There was a key with a piece of paper underneath.

"kruispadstraat 61

PS We replaced the license plate of the car, you can use it now

She started the car again and drove on to the address. The address was an apartment she had always gone to as a young girl when she had run away again; she had been through a lot there. She had broken into it a few times in her younger years when it was vacant and had been deflowered there by her first boyfriend.

Now, where there used to be a house, there was a pizza store with two apartments above.

She parked the car in the designated spot, and putting the key in the keyhole, went upstairs and came to a brown door that was ajar.

She entered a narrow white corridor with three doors on the right and two doors on the left.

The first door on the right was a mixture of a closet to hang and put the coats and shoes. The second door was an average bathroom with a toilet, bathtub and double sink. The third door was of a huge living room with huge windows.

She went back into the hallway and looked at the other two doors, the first closest to the front door was of a bedroom. Inside was a king-size bed with two light brown nightstands and a television hung against the wall at the foot end.

She walked back to the living room, which was set up with the relaxation area to her left, there was a black fabric L-shaped sofa, a sleek black coffee table with some kind of black sheep mat underneath and another large television.

Behind the sofa was the dining room with a simple table and dresser. The windows made the room forget its straight shape and ran like a diagonal from wall to wall, the terrace was so large that it could hold a large table and barbecue and still have plenty of room.

Back inside, she saw an open white kitchen with all the appliances she needed.

There was another key with a piece of paper on the table.

"This is the key to the door up here, then you can always lock the door behind you. There is also a cell phone in your nightstand and your target can be found on it"

She grabbed the key, put it in her pocket and walked to the bedroom. When she started up the cell phone she saw as a screensaver the picture of her father in the chair and for a moment she felt her stomach turn and wanted to throw the phone away, but her will to save him restrained her and so she just went to the messages.

There she saw a name that did make her run to the bathroom, she vomited everything out of her stomach and almost passed out. She ran the shower and washed everything from the prison and feces off her, when she got out she felt clean and reborn only her target was on her stomach.

Her target was none other than John of Braban, it was her father's best friend and he had also been chosen as her godfather. Why would they want him dead? And a better question was: Could she even kill him? He had always been with her for as long as she could remember, and she was seized with guilt.

Tears ran freely down her cheeks for the first time and for the first time in her life she didn't bother to stop them; he was worth some tears.

Don't miss out!

Visit the website below and you can sign up to receive emails whenever Jens Van Wolput publishes a new book. There's no charge and no obligation.

https://books2read.com/r/B-A-HYGV-BUVHC

BOOKS 2 READ

Connecting independent readers to independent writers.

Also by Jens Van Wolput

Achter Baren
Uitbreken voor familie
Achter Baren: Alles Voor Familie

Behind Bars
Escaping for family

Verborgen Passie
Ronde 1: Verborgen Passie

9 798230 690405